Your Body

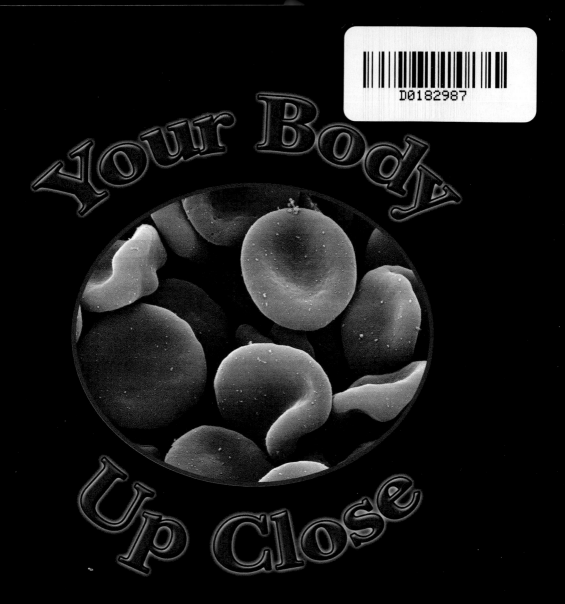

Up Close

Jillian Powell

Contents

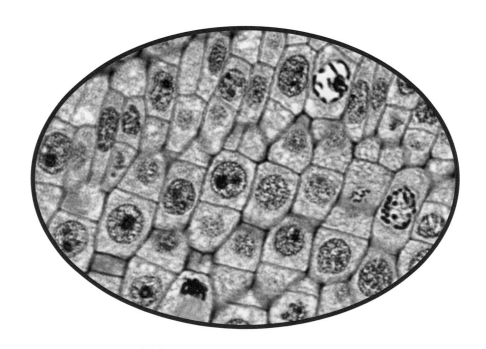

Introduction

Your body is made from millions of tiny parts called
cells. Cells are so tiny that you cannot see them with
just your eyes. You need to use a **microscope**
to see the cells in your body. A microscope
makes cells look much, much bigger.

▼ Some microscopes make cells look
250 000 times their real size!

Chapter 1

Your Skin

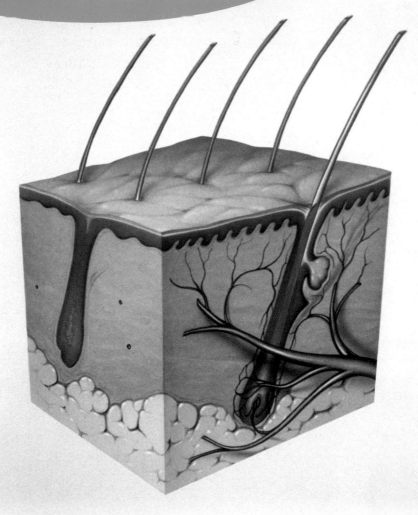

▲ Skin that you see is made of dead cells.

Your skin is made of old and new cells. The top of your skin is made of old, dead cells. Every day, you lose lots and lots of these cells. New skin cells grow under the old cells.

▼ Sweat comes out of the skin through pores.

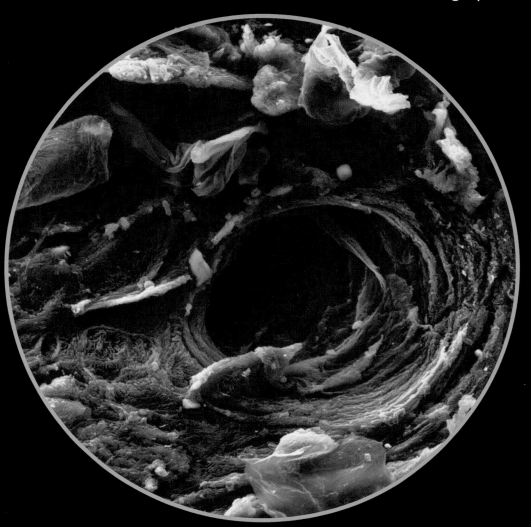

Your skin helps to keep you cool. Skin has tiny holes called **pores**. Every time you get hot, drops of **sweat** come out of each pore. The sweat dries on your skin. It helps you feel cool.

▲ You get goose pimples when you are cold or scared.

If you feel cold or something scares you, you get goose
pimples on your skin. You get goose pimples when tiny
muscles under your skin pull the roots of your hairs.
Each hair then stands up.

▼ Bumpy skin is good for gripping things.

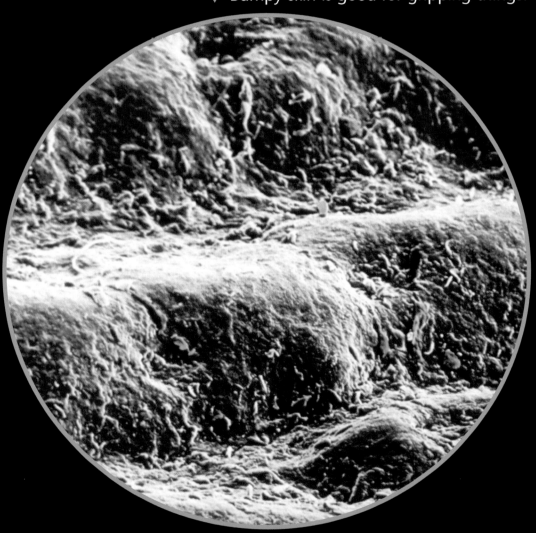

The skin on your hands and feet is thick. This thick skin is made up of lots of little bumps. The bumps help your hands and feet to grip things.

Chapter 2

Your Mouth

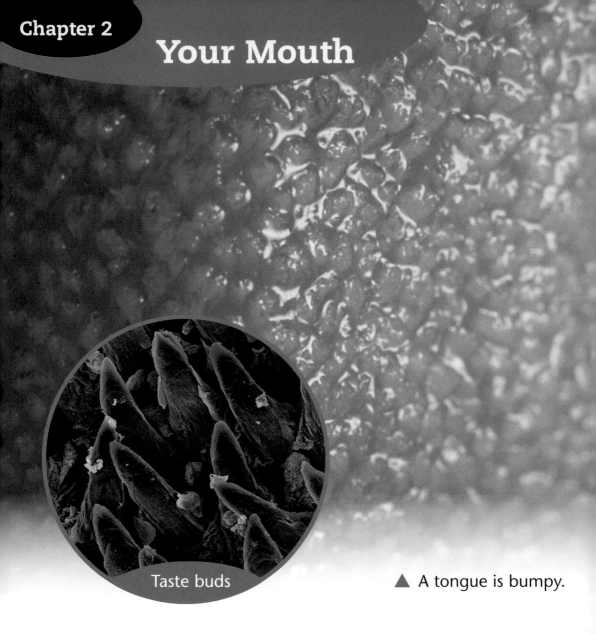

Taste buds

▲ A tongue is bumpy.

Your tongue has lots of tiny bumps on it. Some of these bumps are made of cells called taste buds. Taste buds tell you if something is sweet, sour or salty. Most of your taste buds are on the sides and back of your tongue.

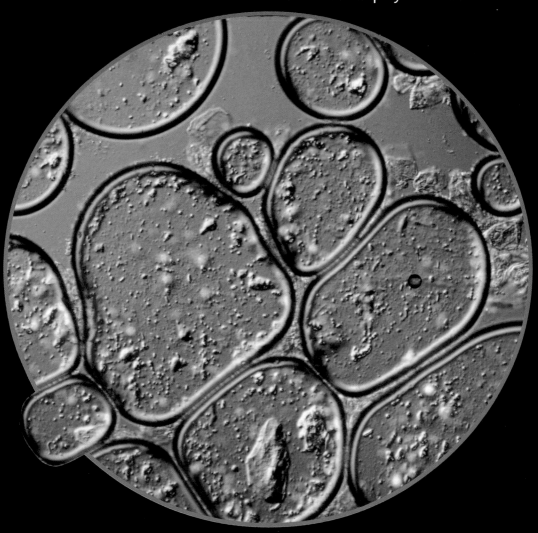

▼ Saliva helps you swallow food.

There is a liquid inside your mouth all the time. This liquid is called **saliva**. Saliva helps you to break down your food and swallow it. Your body makes more than 6 cups of saliva every day!

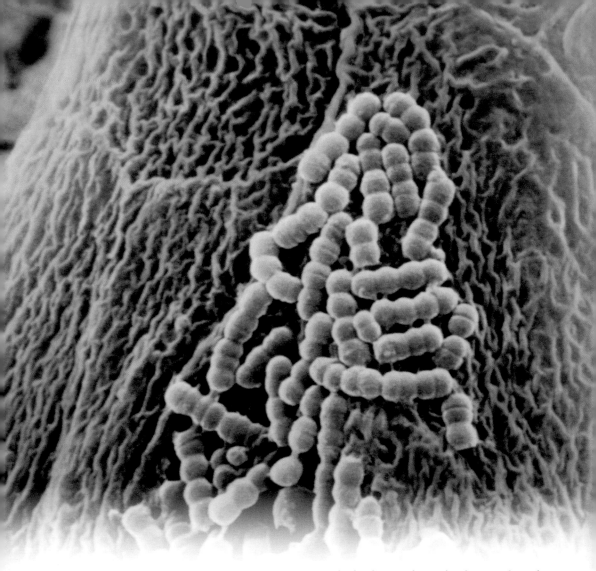

▲ Bacteria in your mouth help to break down food.

There are lots of tiny things living in your mouth. They are called **bacteria**. Most of the bacteria in your mouth keep you healthy. They help to break down the food that you eat.

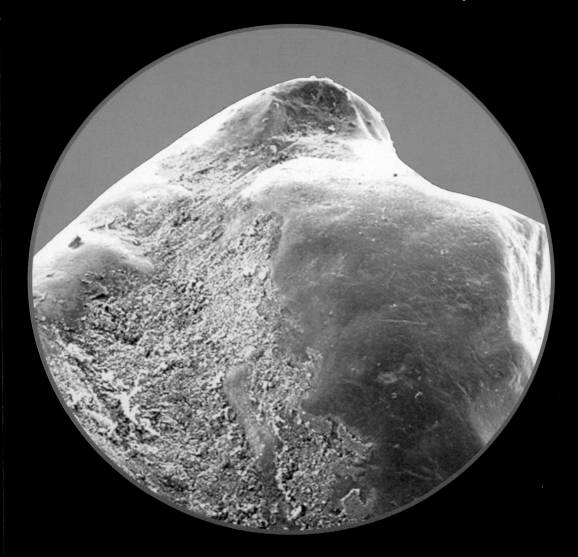

Some of the bacteria that live in your mouth don't help to keep you healthy. They mix with sweet foods and stick to your teeth. They can even make holes in your teeth if you don't brush them.

Chapter 3

Your Eyes and Ears

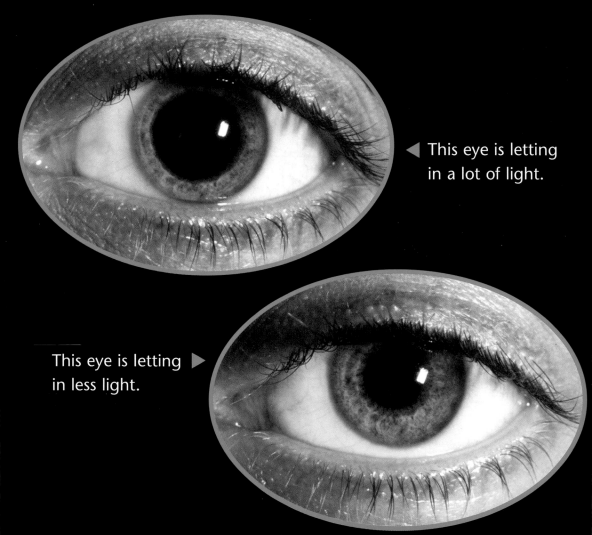

◀ This eye is letting in a lot of light.

This eye is letting ▶ in less light.

Your eyes are made of millions of cells. Some of these cells are muscles. The muscles let light into your eyes. They work to let more or less light into your eyes.

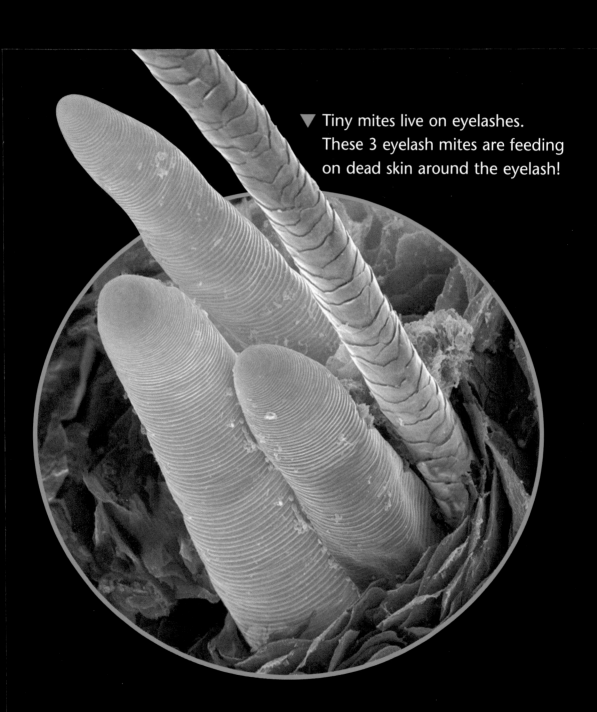

▼ Tiny mites live on eyelashes. These 3 eyelash mites are feeding on dead skin around the eyelash!

Eyelashes are the hairs on your eyelids. Each of your eyes has about 200 eyelashes. They keep dust and dirt out of your eyes.

▲ Some ear cells carry sound.

Inside each of your ears are millions of cells. Special cells in each ear help you to hear. How do they do this? They carry sounds to your brain.

Other cells in your ear help you to keep your **balance**.
These cells are inside tiny tubes filled with liquid. As you
move your head, the liquid moves. The cells move and
send messages to your brain, so it can help you balance.

Chapter 4

Your Hair and Nails

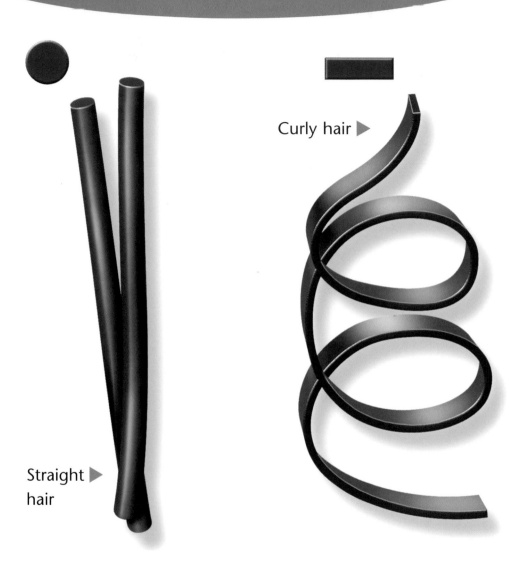

Curly hair ▶

Straight ▶ hair

You have about 5 million hairs on your head and body. These hairs grow out of tiny tubes in your skin. Straight hairs are round and curly hairs are flat.

▼ Hair is made from dead cells.

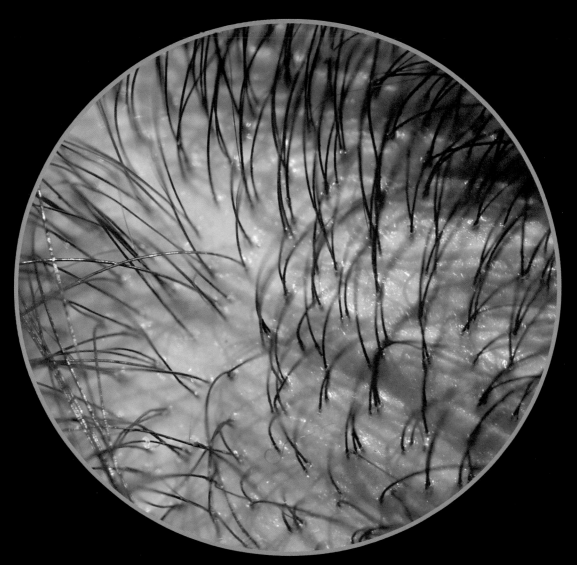

The part of the hair you can see is made of dead cells.
You don't feel anything when you cut it. When old
hairs fall out, new hairs grow back in their place.

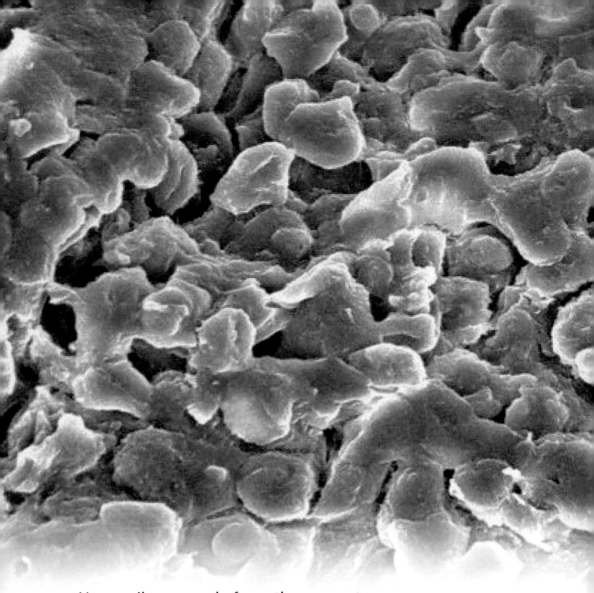

▲ Your nails are made from the same strong
stuff that makes an animal's claws.

The nails on your body are made of cells. Nails keep
your fingers and toes safe from knocks and bumps.
Nail cells are strong and tough.

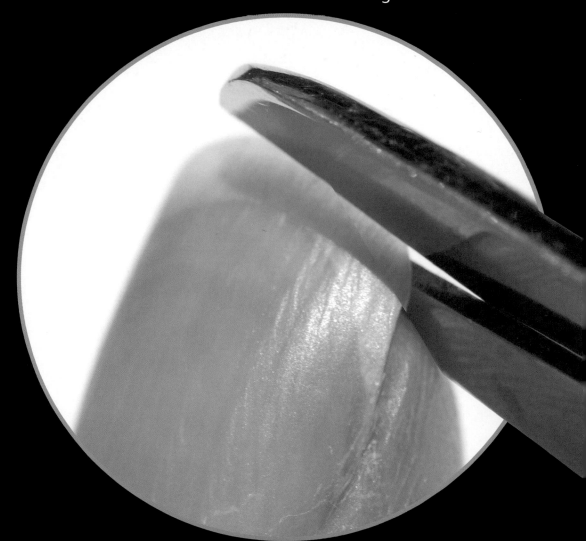

▼ When you cut your nails, you
are cutting off dead cells.

Your nails grow over the tips of your fingers and toes.
The part of the nail that you can see is made from

Chapter 5

Looking at Cells

Microscopes help people to understand how their body works. Doctors use microscopes to see if cells are healthy or not. Doctors can look at blood cells under a microscope.

▼ Doctors can tell if cells are healthy.

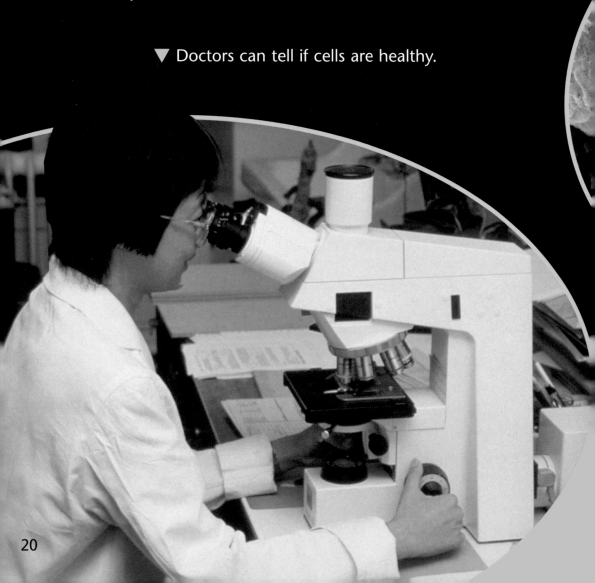

▼ White blood cells fight germs.

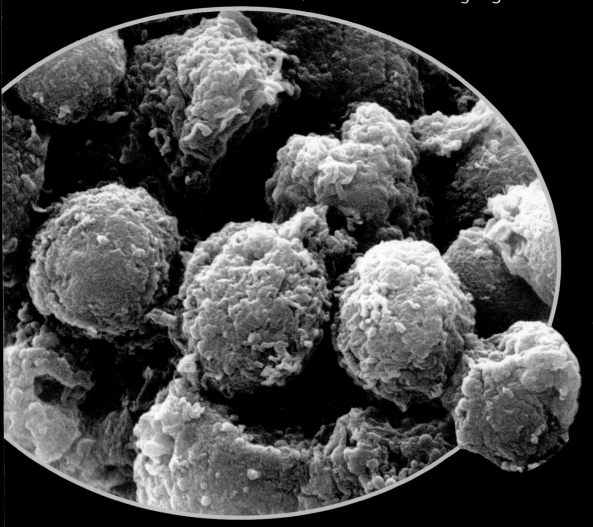

One drop of blood has millions of red and white blood cells in it. The white blood cells work to keep the cells in the rest of your body healthy. They help to fight bacteria. They help to fight other **germs** too.

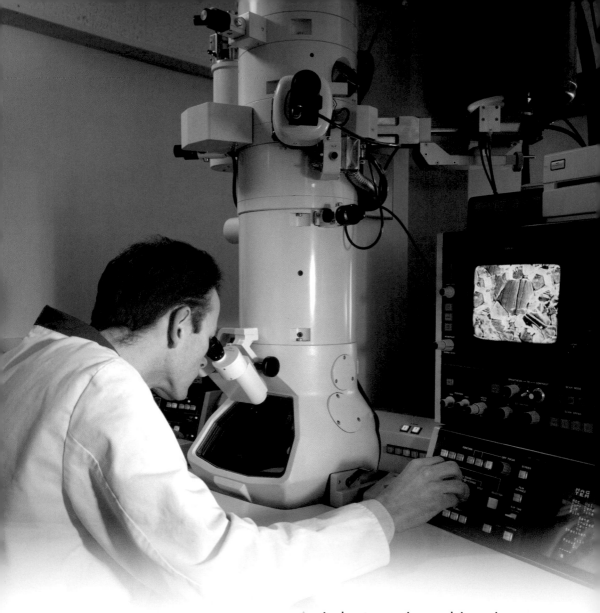

▲ A doctor using a big microscope.

Some microscopes work with computer screens. With these microscopes, you can make things look millions of times bigger than they really are. Now that's up close!

Glossary

bacteria	tiny, one-celled living things
balance	a steady, even position of the body
cells	the tiny units of a living thing
germs	tiny living things that can make you sick
microscope	a tool that makes things look bigger
muscles	bundles of cells that can squeeze and stretch to move parts of the body
pores	tiny holes in the skin that let out sweat
saliva	the liquid in your mouth that helps you to swallow food
sweat	the salty liquid that comes out of your skin pores when you are hot

Index